An
EXMOOR ALBUM

selected by
Joan
Astell

REDCLIFFE
Bristol

First published in 1988
by Redcliffe Press Ltd.,
49 Park St., Bristol.

© Joan Astell

ISBN 0 948265 81 7

The text of this book
has been set in Garamond 11 pt. solid
and captions in Garamond 10pt. solid.

Photoset and Printed by
WBC Print, Bristol

Exmoor—the impossible dream

Western Flying Post of October 8th, 1819: 'Mr Knight has recently augmented his property on Exmoor Forest by the purchase of several thousand additional acres. Under the judicious direction of this gentleman and with his ample fortune this vast and hitherto uncultivated tract of country will shortly assume a new and cheerful character. A handsome residence is in course of erection and great improvements of the soil are in contemplation which from the undoubted fertility of the greater part of this extensive moor will not fail yielding its spirited proprietor a valuable compensation for the liberal expenditure he has bestowed on this neglected district.'

Alfred Vowles' early photographs of Exmoor clearly show the impossibility of John Knight's dream of taming the moor. He purchased the land in 1818, hoping to turn the natural beauty of the wild moorland into a viable agricultural concern. But the moors refused to be tamed and, despite the sinking of shafts for mining copper and iron ore, Knight and successive moorland owners have failed to profit from the land.

In these photographs, Vowles has captured Exmoor's more dramatic scenery, its still almost inaccessible places, lonely farms and villages and tiny remote churches. Vowles visited all these places on foot—he continually shunned the horse and, later, the car. His son, whom I was privileged to meet on a recent rare visit to England from his home in New Zealand, told me that even when indulging his passion for hunting, Vowles ran with the hounds instead of riding.

During the preparation of this book I too have visited these places and found fascinating, not so much the changes but, often, the lack of change—a rarity perhaps in the 20th century.

Joan Astell—Minehead 1988

EXMOOR PONIES TROTTING TO BAMPTON FAIR.

R HEADS AND TAILS AT BAMPTON FAIR.

VOWLES.

Exmoor wild ponies rounded up each October and led to Bampton Fair. The windows of shops and houses had to be barricaded against the frightened ponies being driven among crowds of people for the first time.

ENGLAND'S SMALLEST COMPLETE CHURCH AT CULBONE, SOM.

VOWLES.

Culbone Church stands 400 feet above sea level and is approached by a walk of three miles. The building dates from around 1280, the oak screen from 1400 and the family pew from the 17th century. The spire was added in 1810. The oldest bell is 14th century and is the oldest on Exmoor.

Bury, underneath Haddon Hill near Dulverton. This bridge is over the river Haddeo, a tributary of the Barle. Note the carriages queueing to use the ford.

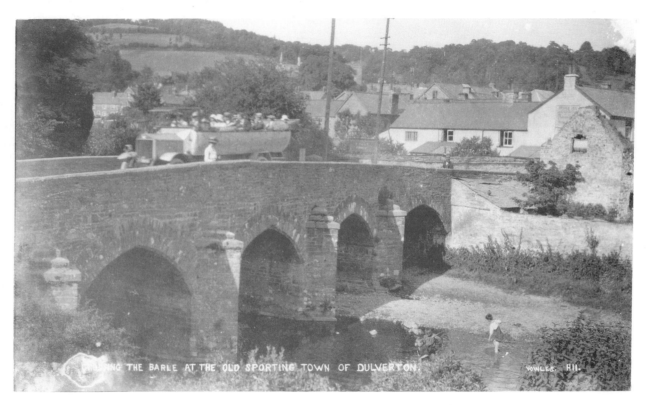

CROSSING THE BARLE AT THE OLD SPORTING TOWN OF DULVERTON. VOWLES. H11.

Dulverton has had its share of flooding and in the year that Lynmouth was destroyed (1952), the river at this spot overflowed with considerable damage.

DUNKERY HILL.

Dunkery Beacon, 1,707 feet above sea level. It is claimed that on a clear day one can see 15 counties from here. This cairn was erected to mark the handing over of Dunkery Hill to the National Trust by Sir Thomas Acland Bt., Col. Wiggen and Allan Hughes.

LYNMOUTH HARBOUR

Lynmouth Harbour.

THE LYN VALLEY AT LYNMOUTH.

D26.

Lynton before the days of the tourist invasion.

The Lounge Hall, The Hoe, Lynton.

Lynton Churchyard. A well posed group of roughs show off the village stocks.

The old village shop. Luccombe.

137

Luccombe, unaltered to this day. Famous for a mass observation survey in the late '30s which is now being updated.

Minehead. The pier, gas works, trippers and the municipal tip—a strange medley for Quay West. The pier was dismantled in 1940.

Minehead. *Emma Louise* dressed over all. The last locally owned trader in the port of Minehead, she carried pit props to the coal fields of South Wales and brought back coal for Minehead's gas works at the harbour.

Minehead. Pip, Squeak & Wilfred, the famous pre-war children's cartoon characters from the *Daily Mirror*, make a real-life appearance.

Combe Sydenham. Once the home of Sir Francis Drake's wife Elizabeth, it is surrounded by legend about the pair's betrothal and long awaited wedding.

The draining of Pinkery Pond was a famous occasion in the search for a William Stenner who disappeared from his home at Riscombe in 1912. To drain it the underground pipe containing two huge plugs had to be located, and approached by a tunnel 60 yards long and less then 3 feet high in places. The dangerous task was accomplished, the water drained out, leaving a sea of black slime, and there was no sign of the missing body. Hundreds of sightseers gathered daily to watch the operation.

The Lynton to Minehead coach descending Porlock Hill in the late 19th century. Excursion fares between the two towns were 8 shillings.

Porlock Weir c. 1935.

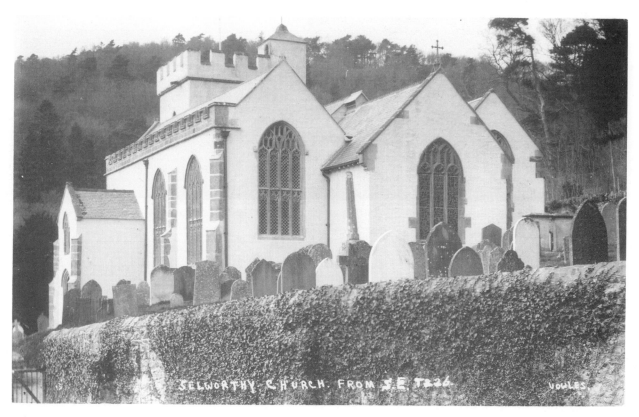

SELWORTHY CHURCH. FROM S.E. T226 VOULES.

Selworthy Church white washed and almost out of place above its thatched village. It can be seen as a landmark many miles across Exmoor.

SHEPHERDS BRIDGE, NR. SIMONSBATH.

Shepherds Bridge, near Simonsbath. The village postman shuns the broken bridge for the safer but wetter crossing.

Tarr Steps Farm. An old British track is said to have crossed the Barle at Tarr Steps.

Washford, The Green Dragon. An early home of Methodism. The house was licensed for preaching in 1795. John Wesley visited Minehead in 1744 and wrote: 'About seven I preached near the sea shore to almost all the inhabitants of that place.'

Webber's Post. An early motor rally.

Wheddon Cross. This is the area for ghost stories, and more abound here than on any part of the moor. The house martin nests in the thatch above the rural filling station. Now renovated, these houses stand at the beginning of the village today.

No. 5. Lorna Doone. Mrs Ridd accuses the Doones of murdering her husband.

The Doone Legend. This card is from Albert Armstrong's 'Picture Play', illustrating the story of Lorna Doone.

Also in this series . . .

Wish you were here!

Old postcards and
photographs of
popular Somerset
holiday resorts

selected by
John
Reynolds